Motiv8ti Publishing
Presents: The Next 30 Days (Volume 1)
My Favorite Yesterday is Today
by
Michael J. Sturdivant

About the Author

Michael Sturdivant is no one in particular. He's a father, a husband, a son, a brother, and a writer. That's my narrative straight no chaser. I am the owner and contributor to Motiv8tionally Speaking LLC. I simply write down affirmations that I truly believe come from God through the Holy Spirit and share them with the world around me. This book is my contribution to a greater movement of transparency and freedom to reach people that want God to find them where they are not where they think they've arrived. Subscribe to Motiv8tionallyspeaking.com for daily affirmations.

Table of Contents

The Next 30 Day

Dedication

This book is dedicated to all the times I was afraid, lied, scared to start and finish what God has placed in my heart to share with those he loved enough to encourage me. To my children, wife, family and friends I love you. Enjoy!

Forward

This book is meant to be read daily. Each entry is meant to inspire you to the degree it makes you reflect and share your experience. It's also not meant to be read alone. This book is meant to be a mental coloring book and your imagination and creativity reflect and define your own perspective that links to the faith you have in God.

You will read both divinely spirited thoughts and the affirmation will follow.

I have learned, time takes no prisoners and never gets tired. Pace yourself with peaceful planning and faithful accountability. Be ready to not be surprised. May the words from these pages impact you to do more than read more once you've finished.

Welcome to the next 30 days of renewal. The intent of this book is to enlighten your spiritual walk. I have been called to share some thoughts that view the world around you while applying some basic and fundamental nuggets. Enjoy and be blessed. Thank you for reading this far. The key to discovering your walk in the "with". Sounds funny but, who you walk with will determine how and when you get there. I walk with God as he orders my steps with grace, forgiveness.

Wherever you may find yourself at this stage in life know that you can do it alone, but the struggle will get easier with God, friends and family to help you along the way. The hard part is knowing you must do this in the loneliness of silence until you understand how God talks to you. It will happen, but one day at a time is how we get there. I would ask that you seek the relationship(s) that allows enough transparency to convict your enough to change without taking the time to wonder who's noticed.

Day 1: The Day God said Hi

I actually met God in between my last lie, my next sin and on the way to my favorite transgression. I had no concept of integrity and my definition of trust was selfish. My glass never full enough. My thirst never hydrated. God's mercy preceded his grace upon the life I had left and suggested hope as a belief. I realized I was no longer talking to myself. God had finally answered a question never asked with an answer I never imagined. I could be anything I desired, but most all free to serve as others willingly in his will.

This thought came to me in the midst of my deepest failure. It was shortly after my second suicide attempt and nothing seemed to be going right. I just wanted to give up on life and every person that was trying to talk sense into me I couldn't hear nor did want to listen. I was not depressed, but I had this desire to stop living before I tried it and failed. I present this as day one because in my lowest moment when I had no more answers God spoke to me through others and I realized I couldn't be anyone, but myself and the pain and agony of knowing that I didn't know where to begin was so scary I shut down.

By this time in my life I was 26 or 27, money wasted, alcoholic, marriage ruined, and I just wanted to take a nap to see if the next day would be different, even I tried the same thing as the day before. The problem was I had developed insomnia and didn't sleep unless exhausted and my body shut down.

Laying there having failed again, I was pretty sure this life was meant to live and all I could wonder is why me and how now. In that moment it happened. Not like bells, fireworks and whistles or anything weird. I heard God say trust me until you can trust you. That was easier said than done. Today is the day it begins. Trust God and in all things put your faith in the actions you can complete without regret. That could be as simple as getting out of bed and being sure that you are out of bed. Allow that to be the most honest and definitive pursuit and use it as motivation to complete sentences. Try this; If I can get out of bed I can go to work and be available to just get through the day.

These first 30 days will be BABY steps. Be kind and patient with your progress but stick with it.

"Amen" is at the end of each affirmation to agree that God gave the words and I never found them to make what you read make sense. Amen.

Day 2: Talking Too Much Saying Nothing

It takes a minute to realize if you've been asked a relevant question or simply sharing a dialogue of hypothetical ideas. God didn't ask for my trust only my faith. I speak life into anything that has the power to believe. The ultimate relief to any question is an answer that can be trusted. We have two ears and one mouth for a reason. We have one mind that can understand that it's aligned to a heart that can break, heal and be overjoyed. The only thing missing is someone to share in the spirit of truth, the curing of laughter, and healing through unconditional requited love. My trust will attract energy that my choices will define as an experience, a season or a cycle. God's plan will reveal his need for my trust. Amen

Voila!!! It's that simple. The path is set your steps will be ordered now adjust your attitude and expectations. First of all, no one knows except you and God what's going on. Find a discreet uninterrupted time to pray and just talk to God, do this consistently. At first it will feel like you talking to the air but focus dig deep and meditate on what your heart truly desires to share with God. Share it without shame, leave it with God and be the best you your transparency can allow. If you want to just be then do so or if you want to share your truth with friends, family or total strangers do so. It's free and will cost you nothing but learning to release the lies that hold you in bondage and will help you receive God's unconditional, relentless, forgiving and understanding love. Amen

Day 3: Keep It Simple and Consistent

My routine is to get up, wash up, dress up, and attack my day as vigilantly as possible. I say thank you to anyone that holds a door, gives me something or helps me along the way. I plan on a mental calendar, talk on the phone and navigate through traffic without making one decision. The traffic moves out of my way before an accident can interrupt my reflexes. I take for granted time, space and wasted energy because they are annoying pet peeves. Yet I do the same. God was not too busy to wake me up. Selfishly I think he thought of me before anyone else. Now that's a relief. I will do better tomorrow I promise I've already planned it. If it's God's will to provide me an opportunity to be grateful. Amen

Plan your day. So, let's review:

1. Trust God until he can trust you.

2. Pray and meditate to communicate with God; when he speaks you will listen to hear.

3. Plan your day. Make a plan to execute all that you must do within the realm of you power, authority and legal rights. No superman antics.

That third task is coming with a caveat. **Put on your plate only what you can handle. Do not volunteer or take on task that you can't.** The best lie we tell ourselves is when we say yes knowing we can't execute or follow through. Give yourself three non-negotiable tasks to complete. Make them "easy peasy lemon squeezy." Quick wins will provide momentum to stick with tougher tasks you will need to accomplish. Amen

Day 4: Wet Bags Strong Arms

Today, let's try to be practical in a spiritual world. Find a paper bag, wet the bottom. Now fill it with your past, all the hurts, disappointments, fears and don't forget the doubt that God heard your humble cry. Next, go out and find some relationships, friendships, "hateships", and "fakeships" to help you carry this wet useless bag into a future you've taken for granted. The problem will not be who you find to help you.

It's always going to be how can one person convince others to carry a wet bottom bag full of worthless substance. The effort it takes to carry this heavy bag is an illusion. When you find a friend that loves and accepts you unconditionally, they don't care about your bag, how many you have, or what's in it.

They wonder why you won't make room for God in your prayer closet. The bag of damaged goods will never leave your thoughts or lead your ambition. It's only available to apply an excuse to the lie you've prepared in advance before you deceive people into thinking you were worth their best effort to simply be a friend. Amen

Leave the past in the past and anyone that judges you for your past can't move into a future God is delivering you into for his will and purpose. People will remember how you treated them and judge what they never had to endure. Your resilience will be the testimony legends are made of. You can't meet failure's expectations when you keep rising to the occasion God can use you to bless others. Amen.

Day 5: A Scar of Redemption

There will be some consistency in everyday activities we fail to recognize. Time is continuous it never gets tired or stops. There will be a day that begins and ends with or without you. People will work together regardless of their differences. God's love will be omnipotent, omnipresent and everlasting. The rules, respect, and honor given to life, love and laughter are not the same for everyone.

We accept patterns of behavior we dignify with attention. We question inconsistency with sarcasm, gossip and insults. Maybe not in that order but they will be recognized, interpreted and judged accordingly. God forgives transgression, trespass and sin with forgiveness. God grants grace without your favor, so you can't deny it. No shower will ever cleanse the gritty feel of guilt.

That's the scar. It will leave a mark that you remember how it got there. It will be deep enough to leave a permanent touch that obedience ignored to recognize before the honest mistake was made and you can't undo it. Redemption scrapes away guilts residue to reveal a new being. Be anyone God can heal, restore and bless. The old you will remind you how far you've come. Amen

You can do anything once there will be an impact that affects those around you or against you. **The mistake is remembered by those who need you to forget that healing leaves the scar but heals the wound from the inside out.** Amen

Day 6: This Hand I Hold

In order to hold a hand there's a commitment to touch, grip, clasp and hold. If you should choose to then take a walk there is a determination to walk and talk together. Steps can be in unison regardless of which leg you, but never out of sync. Before a word is spoken someone must take the lead. Someone must allow a lead to be taken. Regardless of the number of steps taken it's done together. God will never leave of forsake you once you give him your hand, a commitment, and the humility to be led. Amen

It takes a lot to acknowledge when you need help. Hands are meant to be held. You are meant to be led. **Reach for God's hand reaching to receive you once you asked him to lead you.** There are three components to this one request. The **need** from within to be vulnerable enough to faithfully submit to a God that you can't see. Can you reach with the **trust** of your heart to feel something you've never felt before? Finally, can you be led by the virtue of your **obedience** to go where God is leading you without hesitation or second guessing.

The feeling you will receive may be in the form of a chill when affirmation meets testimony. God will speak to you through someone else's need. The funny part is that you will talk yourself out of helping someone you could easily bless by doubting you are worthy. Have you asked to be led and are you willing to hold on as he leads?

Trees bear fruit even if no one eats them. Do you have fruit to bear or are you a stick in a forest of trees jealous that you could grow better fruit than a tree that has not been planted yet. The hand can do anything without an intentional spirit. Your hands are meant to be filled with something between air and the desires of you heart. Allow God to put his love into your hands. Amen

Day 7: Transparent Integrity

I have learned to celebrate everyday as if it was my last. I don't waste words, time or energy. It can seem boring, lazy and monotonous to anyone else except me. I'm at peace after going through a hell I created. My hell didn't have a devil with horns or heat I couldn't resist. I never intended for my transparency to change anything for anyone else. My opinions should not shape your view or validate perceived facts. **I pray that at the end of the first seven days you've given God the opportunity to meet you where you're at.** Life gives opportunities starting with a first breath. God gives life everlasting through a relationship shaped by your trust, faith and the desires of your heart. Amen.

Day 8: To Prey or Not to Pray

The prey and the predator do not decide who's on first. One becomes the other and the cycle either ends or begins all over again. Accept Christ once and pray that predators resist the temptation of your humility, charity, and favor. Their diets thrive on haters, cynics, and pessimist. Prey relies on survival instincts, luck, and timing. There will always be enough prey for predators. Praise gives every prayer the energy to survive any predator's attack and expectation of an easy meal. Survival has no winners or losers. There are just days that you stay hungry and deliberate in your pursuit to find what you hunger desires and your risk can manage. Amen

Faith carries a risk that your expectations will not be met. It will not feel good, but each testimony will look exactly the same. It will all work out. God will show up in the midst of chaos and quiet to calm the storm and your doubts. Ask a divorcee if the demise of their marriage was because they were both happy and their expectations were met with delivered promises. God's promise is that your sins were and are forgiven. God loves you unconditionally with two expectations: Love him with your mind, body and soul and love one another without reservations. Pray for your haters. They are working hard to find reasons to hate you even if there aren't any.

Day 9: Fed Up

"Fed" has a last name, "Up". He's often given a middle name people use to make him sound important. Everyone says hello to Fed Up. Fed Up has a dear friend. They call her "Sick". Her real name is Ann. Her last name was "Tired". Everyone please wave at Sick Ann Tired. Fed Up and Sick Ann Tired stared at the floor of a four-sided box with no bottom on a street called desire. They stand in their box holding hands looking at the square floor they share. Everything outside the box represents a past fear that put them in a similar place they've seen before. Each disappointment reinforced a side of the box they have never seen. Their emotions made the space feel bigger while their lack of faith added familiar details to a problem God had already solved.

They finally asked each other who told them they had to stay in this box or any box for that matter. Fed bowed his head to pray while Ann called on the Lord. Fed Up separated his hand from Sick Ann Tired's grip. She never realized how much they held each other back from God's will. Fed walked toward a wall he could never touch while Ann opened a door that was never shut. They lost touch but stayed connected in Christ. They met at a crossroads called Delivered and Set Free where they lived in everlasting life.

When you are set free, stay free. Don't test to see if God was serious about your salvation. If the taste of liquor, cigarettes or infidelity have been taken out of your spirit don't bring them back into existence. Yesterday is in the past for a reason. You will never get it back and it can't change anything today. It happened, and you survived. Be free to learn from the experience without reliving the sentiment.

Day 10: The Lies Impressions Tell

There's this internal judgement that some things will never change. Even if they do it's a fluke coincidence. You are still who I always thought you were. If your expectation is to be disappointed by the effort that achieves failure in your view of their potential, check ya' self as quick as possible. That's a powerful revelation of entitlement that one should be careful about utilizing to hold others accountable.

You fail until you succeed, and the heavy part is that none of us live for one another. We live out of the survival of those first two elements that attracted parents to coexist to trust one another to conceive you in ideal, on purpose or mistake. If you can survive birth living should get easier. The worst thing we can do is to be grown trying to impress someone that will never understand what it took for you to get here. Here will always be the middle. If I met you, today we in the middle deciding if and to what degree we can connect. If we hit a tough patch and know we want the relationship.... we in the middle of making our lives better.

The point is that if God doesn't judge me based on who I think he is. He trusts me based on the deliverance we've grown through together. Pleasing people will give me recognition that won't get me into heaven. Love has no specificity it accepts the salad for the nutrients it provides, not the diet that never works.

When someone finally impresses you be mindful that your approval is an acknowledgement of fears you've never had to live with. You either uplift or tear down someone; hurt people only know how to hurt people. They don't get good at inflicting pain on the helpless people that want to love them in spite of their own flaws. They make more people that feel it's necessary to make people earn their behavior as a rite of passage. In the end they become religious to validate the hell they take others through. God can't protect you from you. He will leave you in the spirit of your efforts to seek attention from people that don't know any better.

Eventually people see you from a mile away and won't entertain the crazy. You know if this applies to you if when a child of God enters the room and you react to the perfection God just presented with judgement. God's watching how you treat his children. They are protected, covered and approved to be where he has led them to serve. How about you? Amen.

Day 11: Outside In

My fears of failure are outweighed by a persistent angst that "someone" wished I could at least once. I have the worst luck coincidence could have ever created. I'm not perfect, patient or proud, just paranoid. I prayed the wrong prayers hoping God knew what I meant. He showed me my low SELF esteem was my issue not his problem. My habits validated my haters sentiment, and nobody cared that I kept saying I didn't have one.

God revealed he created me perfectly to believe salvation was mine through him. I forgot that I had to forgive myself to trust it was true. I invited him into my life without making space where I needed him most; my heart, mind and soul. I wanted everyone to see God on my outside without letting him in. **God fulfills doubtful spaces from the inside out. God didn't want my apology, just a complete yes. I had to replace hate with love and complacency with living.** I still fail at my own expectations, but God never showed me where I didn't meet his. Amen

Day 12: Who Lied to You

You will never catch a liar before he believes his truth. The art of deception is better than the reality of peace, to them. "Delayed chaos with the promise of confusion" is the liar's credo. Who has ever met a lie that didn't sound good. It's not the words or the tone, but the lie itself that hurts. It didn't touch you, but you feel your trust crucified without a cross to bear. The same as fingerprint leaves an undeniable impression, lies separate the body from others trust. God can heal any hurt, but trust requires redemption.

God forgives people don't. Lies invent creative consequences that never existed. A lie can be told anywhere except in prayer. God will provide the desires of your heart. Your spirit will prepare the body to receive exactly what you requested. A blessing in or a blessing out will remove the temptation to try. Amen

Day 13: Power

Words have the power to focus your mind on an anticipated message or concept that achieves meaning. If you can read, then understanding becomes a matter of context. People are minds, spirits and bodies confirmed by experiences that provide a trade-off that works for them specifically. The context of maturity exists to ensure growth can align consistent behavior. The body reacts to stimuli. The mind is intrigued.

The spirit yearns to be nurtured. When the body hurts the mind searches for any alternative desire the spirit can accept to believe the healing is available. Trust God to the degree, healing will occur or being with him will cure all sickness. Either way the testimony will change someone in a way they never realized was possible. Amen

Day 14: Hamster Wheelin'

No matter how fast you run on the hamster wheel of life you will get no further than the wheel moves fast. The harder you run the more momentum you build to run in place, but never progress. The same ole same ole regardless of the effort. The words may change but the message is the same. The last sentence is just like the next until you understand the difference between process and progress.

The difference between being held captive and being a distraction is simple. **The maturity it takes to let go or not be as needy as your dependence will define your growth. Faith inspires before it motivates to engage an action. Actions speak louder than words so move when God speaks to your situation.** IF God says duck ask him why on the floor.

The temporary condition of one circumstance can keep you chasing yesterday's trouble hoping for a new today. The habits that hold us back are the walls to the cage. The self-destructive cycles we create are the hamster wheels we choose while chasing a dream that didn't require sleep. God wants you conscious enough to recognize his blessing without you choosing your option first. There are no regrets when you know where God is, and you aren't. There's a door to every cage. The goal is to not place walls around God's plan when your faith is the key. Amen

Day 15: Memories

Memory's accusations are so deliberate they remember the past way better than faith's future. Whether positive or negative memories name the guilty, shame the innocent and leave you out of conflicts blame. **The best memories skip the small to details to foreshadow the good that could only be possible through sanctification.**

We all have a choice to see the brighter side of a cloudy day tomorrow or accept that the possibility of rain will leave something wet. Rains specific timing is unpredictable, yet we know it will not last forever. The day is never ruined because of rain. Your attitude makes the day all you expect it to become. God gave you a day you couldn't ask for, predict, begin or end. You only choose how it will go. Amen

Day 16: Sideline Saints

It's easy to be self-righteous when you can't remember the last time you needed anyone or lacked for anything. A lot of people haven't, and some will never admit that they desire acceptance and peace more than money. You may have never broken one law or commandment, but you're still not perfect or satisfied with anything good or positive in your own life.

Sideline saints co-sign on others demise before God's favor can intercede to soften the blow. **The fall is never a tragedy just a moment we wish we could change after it was too late.** Judgement is the actual crime. Shame is the timeless sentence a victim feels. The actions of the fallen will be vilified by those who know no better and have never made their specific mistake. Sideline saints have never honestly experienced grace or accepted mercy. These are the people you pray for every time you hear them gossip about and to you. If you're in the game of life there will be celebrations, losses and timeouts taken.

Sideline saints only know how to throw flags at an approach to life they'll never attempt. God does not keep score or statistics. He measures what happens on the down you accept him. It only matters how sincere your heart is when asking him to take the finish this game of life and forgive you of your sins. Every play after that will be successful. Allow him in the huddle to call the plays. Amen

Day 17: Talking to Myself

There is a separate level of transparency I'm willing to share with friends, family and strangers. Not everyone will have the same level of access or intimacy. Some access is reserved for the part of my truth you can understand, accept, or adjust to existing within.

The scope of each relationship has a level of relevance based on time invested, truths accepted, and the tolerance of differences. You can't choose how family will judge you or how well you think a friend should know you. Strangers on the other hand could easily be disguised as a transparent blessing that can only bless you with an opportunity to listen as bad as you need to share.

You can tell a lot about a stranger, because you judge them as you approach their perceived vulnerability. **Strangers don't appear by chance or coincidence they are placed in your path for a genuine experience.** What we say about strangers is actually how we see ourselves only out loud, so God hears us both. The superficial person we think we are and the angel we judge. BE mindful how you treat strangers. They are people that God has protected from your insensitive judgement. Be the highlight of their day so they can tell someone how good God was to them. Amen

Day 18: To Slick to Slip

One cold DC morning I parked on a sheet of ice. At the time it looked appealing and available to my needs. It was still a sheet of ice. Selfishly, I found the closest parking spot near my office. I noticed no one else had parked there, which as strange especially on a cold day like this. I was willing to feel lucky this day. My first thought was there is my blessing, thank you Jesus.

That first step getting out of the car gave me great sense of confidence. No sooner than I closed the locked door and adjusted my backpack, swoosh. I went down hard and fast. I had fallen against my locked car door and all I could think was I'm falling to fast to catch myself. I was telling myself to tuck and roll, but the ice didn't listen. My knee, my side, my elbow then my head made hard quick painful contact with that searing cold ground. I had cool points to save, so I tried to get up really quick, but remember I hit my head and I was dazed and confused about which way was up and that ice kept laughing at me.

I had to take some deep breaths and roll till I got to the not so icy part and pick myself up, like a boss. I looked around and everyone laughing hysterically as they drove by was now gone. It was meme worthy to say the least. How could I find a great parking spot that blessed me to be that close only to fall when I thought it was safe to take a step God was ordering. Man did I misread the signs.

I didn't fall getting out my car or lose cool points getting into the building. It's the in between that gets you every time. I kept thinking about how the ice could thaw if the temperature raised a few degrees. I knew God could do that much in a days' time. It got colder, roads got slicker, and yes it started to sleet. They even allowed us to leave early to beat the bad weather coming. As I walked to the parking lot, I noticed my entire car was on frozen. I realized my dilemma and understood the sign. **God can't change the arrogance or ignorance you place your trust in and call that part faith.** I expected God to transfer the ice to water because he could. I could have been patient and selected a better place to chill. Amen

Day 19: The Difference Between Me and God

I don't know what inspired Jesus to become a carpenter or even if he was the best. I've worked at less than my full potential for full pay my entire career. For some reason, he's always insulated my incompetence with people that trusted me more than I believed in myself.

I don't know how he divided 2 fish and 3 loaves of bread between all those people, but it was enough. My family has never gone hungry. Even when I didn't have it all or some God made a way. I had to borrow money or not pay a bill and my own ignorance caused debt God had already forgiven.

I know he asked his father to forgive the people killing him. I wouldn't. I know he was crucified for my sins. I know he's the truth and the light. I can barely remember my old lies, so I don't tell new ones. I know he rose on the third day. I have a hard time laying my burdens down. I forgive but forget so slow that I remember details better than the role I played in the problem. I have condemned other with no remorse or retort. I'm human, he was the son of God.

So, there you have it the difference between me and God. Over time I have let it all go. I was saved but it took time to allow deliverance to show. I can do all the things that I have in the past except promise my children tomorrow, not mine or theirs. I can tell them to be smart knowing I never felt smart even when I achieved straight A's and the honor roll and entire school year. I can set the example. I had to realize that I can be who God has told me I am.

I am…a child of God, a son, a father, a servant, a protector and everything God has trusted me to become when I stopped worrying about what I wasn't without him. Eventually we realize we're not God, but his representatives that make heaven on earth for those he allows us to serve and lead back to him, so they can understand that they can't compete with the greatest unconditional love they fight feeling.

Day 20: Brake Light Promises

Before them there was just time to waste, money to burn and dreams to defer. I was not born under the same circumstances nor would I try to change theirs. I thought this was all a miracle until I became a father and husband.

Now I get up before them to prepare and assure their ride to school is safe. I need God's protection over the road to lead the way. The ride is forty-five minutes door to door. I want them to sleep a little more. I want them to hear the gospel music and its message while they rest. I don't want them to know how sleepy I am. I'm the driver and they are my precious cargo. I'm focused, tired and need to get them there by certain time too.

There will be times I can't make every light and that'd be great. There will be times when the weather is great and every cars cruising at 78. I just hope our prayer will be answered to arrive back home sometime today. There's just one thing I taught them to do. I told them to enjoy the view but pay attention to the brake lights ahead. All of sudden someone way ahead stopped abrupt. I reached my arm across my sons lap while pressing on the brakes. God controlled the cars behind us and we arrived late, but safe. Amen

There will be times you are driven to lead when you wonder how when you have never been equipped. The gas pedal has a mentality, like the car is to a person wanting to do right. As long as your foot is on the gas the car should move forward. Depending upon the traffic you will feather the gas pedal to regulate the car's tempo to manage how well you control the vehicle. God is doing all the pressing. The speed is dictated by the obedience you intend to maintain in what is posted, your confidence in your ability and your fear in getting a ticket or an accident.

God won't keep you out of an accident, but the respect you have in the trust you display will allow you an opportunity to see things before they happen. God will give you sight unseen in ways you never anticipated.

Day 21: Fists Tight

You ever squeezed your fist so tight your hands felt weightless. You ever had a knot in your throat so big you couldn't speak. You ever been too hurt to scream or disappointed to yell about it. That's the moment your eyes well up and one tear escapes. It's like your entire body is a pressure valve that finally leaks. Every emotion is clamoring to escape.

God is allowing the wasted emotion to hemorrhage on the inside to come out through your tear ducts not your eyes. You can't cry quick or drown in your own tears, but the heart can be broken. The pain can be indescribable. You don't care who sees you but they're too afraid to look directly at you. God is watching the drama unfold. He's not counting tears just waiting for you to give whatever breath you have left all to him. Your fist slowly open. Your face is now dry. You can laugh at every ugly cry face selfie and know that God heard you and fixed it you in mind.

Your faith and trust will find you time only God can provide to make the best decision that trust's in HIM. When the blessing is revealed, and favor is confirmed you'll laugh every time you see the devil trying to bate you into hitting something that can't fight back. Amen

Day 22: Sense is not Common

None of my senses have anything in common. They must all work together to create synergy. I can see what I hear and feel a difference only if I believe what I selfishly perceive. My beliefs are channeled through an experience only I understand, but others may relate. Arrogantly my senses perceive attitudes. I don't know which sense gets agitated first, when or how.

I can tell when I refuse to allow God to handle my enemy's frustration with his grace in my blessings. When I try to explain it only arguments arise. The effort to get a point across is defeated by their sense of righteousness, because I'm never at fault. We're too loud to be wrong so we keep talking at one another without listening. **God gave us all five senses and a choice to love in spite of our shortcomings.**

How we use our senses to love, forgive, and praise will be different, but affect everyone we encounter. Physically our bodies will function the same life through death. Our senses will be responsible for interpreting how we treat one another. A relationship requires only two to communicate. A rumor only needs one perception without any common sense to ruin it. God never made one assumption about you. He was sure he loved you before you were ever a thought and designed you perfectly to serve others. Amen

Day 23: So, IT's Happening

I'm at this stage in life where IT is happening. I didn't know when it would begin but I complained about IT not being all that it should have been when God showed me what I prayed for in detail. IT didn't shock me, but I was irritated that I didn't ask for more or at least been more specific in the details. I wasn't winning or losing, just living with two regrets. IT never cared as much as I did about all the attention it invested in other's interest. They had mutual exclusive trouble that they constantly stayed in struggle to fix.

My lack of focus on where God was leading my life distracted me from being invested, interested, or committed. I looked for all the trouble I found when I was young, and it taunts me as I walk past it daily. I grew bored with the predictability of its antics. Nothing creative just the same ole same. The regret is knowing I wasn't special to IT. Trouble didn't care about the consequences that I've had to endure over the past 20+ years of retribution, reconciliation and recovery. IT was an equal opportunist.

IT forced me to follow rules my sin created, and my emotions entertained. I'm civil now and responsibility tells me how much trouble I can afford and how much costs too much. When you think of the freedom you have available to make a difference versus the responsibility that comes with the blessing, some will see IT clearly. Some will wait for IT to just happen, IT DOESN'T. Others genuinely take the initiative to BE all that GOD has called them to be.

There is a fundamental confidence that come with their faith as they grow and mature. Those on the outside looking in feel some sorta way about how do you (specifically) have the right to be who, where, and how you are. As you achieve, they complain. As you succeed, they hope you stumble. If you fall, they are mad that you didn't fail completely.

The whole while you pray that they know HIM sooner than WHEN and HOW he found you. When the power of your faith shows in your attitude, humility exudes gratitude. Doors will open to new opportunities to show your transparent beauty and favor. Beauty is in the eye of the beholder. I know he is watching over me BECAUSE I stay focused on HIM not IT. Amen

Day 24: Friendship

The hardest people to love is those that forget that their sins were forgiven before they betrayed your trust. They remember why they betrayed you but can't understand your disappointment. You're hurt that you accepted the behavior thinking you were the exception to their rules. The sad part is that you probably never knew there was a score being kept managing the friendship. It's obvious when one friend needs another friend to feel they are the better individual.

If you think you are the better of best friends, then you're the friend keeping score that lost. Friends serve each other through humility. Jealousy, envy, and disloyal deeds end friendships that never had a chance. Enemies are guilty of being the perpetrator of betrayal. Your enemy will reveal itself through actions you witness them execute in other managed friendships. Their snide comments are refined truths they need to set-up an unassuming victim. Your opportunity to escape the Devil's snare closes when you sit, watch and can be entertained by the outcome. Sin knows your temptation and waits to grab your attention. It's subtle before it becomes blatant and relentless in making you accept this is who you really were the whole time. That's the worst lie a lot of people pass from generation to generation.

God will send help to align his will to change your ways upon request. Help and helpers serve as a voice of reason that answers your questions and calms your fears with the word of God. Their struggles will seem less of a battle once you stop competing with their submission to God. Friendships will last a season when the relationship requires competition and entertainment. Friendships last a lifetime when we know God is the father and we serve and respect each other like sisters and brothers. Amen

Day 25: I Leave Mean People Be

I leave mean people alone because their truths disrupt my happiness. The fool in me wants to convince them that the other side of the pillow is cooler than the hot head laying on it. I have problems the same as they do, just none are self-inflicted anymore. I know my cheerful disposition is the last thing they wanna see on the same sidewalk. I'd walk backwards to avoid their bitter looks, but then I'd look stupid watching them watch me walk away looking at me crazy. We still have to pray for those with anger, resentment, and entitled attitudes looking to abuse one of God's children.

I remember praying and fasting hoping God would punish them for scaring me. I was shocked when nothing happened. I had the nerve to ask God to reveal his power to dispose of a threat I perceived, while he covered me. There looks were dirty and body language funky. God gave me every option and a clue that this was someone that needed him more than me. After walking backwards and watching an opportunity to speak life silently into another person's life I realized we both lacked the joy of peace. **Peace will struggle as long there is someone willing to fight God's attempts to love you through your judged imperfections.** Amen

Day 26: God Never Told Me NO

It took me a while to realize God never told me "no" I just disagreed with most of his "yeses". Yes, I can forgive, I just don't forget. Yes, I am saved, but I don't want to be delivered from "everythang" all at once or next week. Some of bondage's binds aren't tight enough to make me regret testing God's grace when only because I assumed the devil had mercy to spare. We must remember the devil is a name caller. It's not what he calls you, but your triggers and how often you answer. A simple "huh" is all he needs.

Your attention span embraces your experience in the name of the sin you try to hide from being exposed. The name calling is an associated microcosm of how you display your doubt to be blessed by God directly. The devil didn't give me a rope to place around God's trust in my strength to be resilient after his answer. I found a scraggly piece of rope to play with during a moment I felt it was rejection. I picked it up because it was labeled trouble, not in the braids but on each cuff attached to the ends. I placed my hands in each one and pulled tight and worried when I felt trapped, when they felt tight.

I realized there was no key to unlock trouble's grip. Even in frustration I couldn't break this rope that was being pulled wherever the devil needed me to create confusion. The devil had me and I was to blame; ashamed, needy and vulnerable. A "hot mess" is what they called me. I couldn't laugh or provide a slick lip reply. The pressure became too much, and the guilt was literally killing me. I fell one day hoping to die and God showed me where he was when I picked up that rope. He was with me the whole time because I believed he died specifically for my sins selfishly. Even though I was saved I've needed God to rescue me from me. Faith and obedience will protect your mind and heart from believing anything the devil may call you. Amen

Day 27: Counting Excuses to Validate Failure

I've made 14 excuses today, 15 were necessary. I didn't waste a lie, I avoided some truths. I trusted some insecurities that warranted a pass. I survived faking through my entire day without being exposed. It started with some subject verb agreement and a misplaced comma, I knew better but was too lazy to shorten an unnecessary sentence.

Then I remembered God said keep your prayers specific and brief. I just wanted to wear my victim badges of righteousness, courage and pity. I was no longer ashamed of circumstances I didn't create. I can't commit to fixing a past I didn't plan. I can only plan for a future God and I agree upon. I've left him where I no longer needed him in a place where emotional decisions explained rational motives.

There were innocent victims that captured untrue parts of my character not my spirit. We loved being undeniable and insignificant critics to a hidden truth that couldn't be hidden. We often disagree, but obedience prevails. I did what they asked and none of it added to their growth. If one person can relate help me understand. I no longer beg for mercy, now I whine about the sufficient grace God has already provided.

I'm the body builder worried about how much my passion weighs knowing my gains only need to be positive. God knows my heart, but my mind races. I hear what's said and react to everything untrue. That's why they judge me, and I answer to the label I'm addressed yet I'm the only one going nowhere. Misery may love company, but they accept one another. **Time, patience and opportunity wait on each other; especially when none are ready to be accepted as valued participants to life everlasting past your doubts.** Amen

Day 28: Arguing with the Reflection of My Expressions

There is an awesome intelligent disagreement between who I think I am and what God saw in creating me. There's one true me, one true you; God knows both and whom we try to fool. We don't know each other just who we think we are to each other. Marriages have a lifetime or a divorce to figure who they disappoint or accept as genuine.

Here's the secret to serenity. The sin you judge God may not convict in your heart, mind or predisposition. Yet when you are convicted to change, we do so once we have a guarantee. The guarantee is that we can sacrifice the consequence necessary for a better existence. I never thought I could sacrifice my decree of confidence for a degree of freedom. Faith and obedience provide a freedom incomparable to any lie ever lived. At one point and time I hoped every lie would be believed, they protected a shameful truth.

The truth is short sweet and complete. It says exactly what it means. No matter how low my low went I could reach my hand above the water my head was under. I expected God to bless my mess or relieve my stress. I held my breath in 4ft of water. I'm 5'10. I've always stooped to a lower level to meet an easier compromise. God's grace allowed me to stand on his promise. We must learn to trust when promises are true, they're delivered on time for you to witness. **When you trust that God is for you and know the lies count against your freedom; life gets easier to live without regrets. Amen**

Day 29: Finding Peace

I pray that each of us finds peace. There are moments that God will catch your attention and keep you focused. A place where laughter replaces heartache and blissful rest consumes all of your weariness. There will be constant reminders that you can't plan your blessings or pick who blesses you. I am grateful for the quiet times when there was no one to blame. Accountability has become my mirror. I can appreciate the light that keeps nothing hidden. I am at peace and enjoy every moment to just say thank you.

Amen

Day 30: Those 3 Types of People

Be aware of 3 types of people:

Those with no purpose.

Those that hurt you on purpose.

Those that use your purpose to enable their sense of entitlement.

God has a purpose for your life, seek it. Our children feed off our initiative and motivation to help them in a time of need. Show them the difference between purpose and entitlement. You are entitled to praise HIM for and thru the sacrifices made for them. Your purpose is to make a difference in the miracle of life through the power of the tongue. What they hear about them is who they believe and eventually become. Hope that they are listening and understand the prayers you believe are for their future.

After the Last Day of Your New Beginning

So, we've made to the end. Prayerfully the past 30 days have given you a renewed perspective. I hope that these affirmations have been fulfilling and have allowed you to see God working in the midst of your relationship with him.

The key is developing that relationship in full transparency. The vulnerable portions will reveal themselves through the release of hurts and unforgiveness. No one can give you the relationship that God wants with you.

The word "with" is so powerful in our day to day lives. The "with" means that you are in this is space called life together. No judgement or throwing your flaws in your face. The things we face with God on our side are better than doing it alone.

I know what it's like to be alone, lonely, and desperate to be accepted. I never truly felt accepted without the condition(s) for what I could do for others. As a child I acted out and isolated myself a lot because it was the safest place for me to escape. We learn what love is initially by what we are told. I was often told I was loved after physical or verbal abuse. Love became a reason. Until I learned what "with" meant I never loved anything or anybody.

This 30 day of perspective is meant to push you toward examining your thoughts and if they are aligned with God's vision for your steps to get closer to others through him. When you think that it's about you; life will show you how selfish it can honestly get. Thanks for reading.

Made in the USA
Middletown, DE
30 May 2019